Up, Up and Away

Written by Sue Graves

Collins

The red balloon goes up, up and away.

It goes over the house.

It goes over the river.

7

It goes over the mountain.

It goes over the sea.

11

The red balloon goes up, up and away!

A Flow Chart

:paw: Ideas for guided reading :paw:

Learning objectives: understand and use terms about books and print: cover, illustration, word, letter, title; match spoken and written words; hear and say initial phonemes in words; ask and answer questions and offer suggestions.

Curriculum links: Knowledge and Understanding of the World: Observe and find out about features of the natural world

High frequency words: the, up, and, away, it, over, house

Interest words: journey, balloon, goes, river, mountain, sea

Word count: 36

Resources: white board and pen

Getting started

- Ask the children to look carefully at the front cover. How many words are there in the title? Point to each word, and read. Encourage the children to use the correct terms *title* and *cover*.

- Discuss what the book is about – a runaway balloon's trip over land and sea.

- Walk through the book and ask the children to discuss where the balloon goes.

- Ask the children to point to the word *goes* on each page. What sound or letter does it starts with? Ask them which words are repeated, e.g. *It goes over the...*

Reading and responding

- Encourage the children to read the book independently in a low voice up to p13. As the children read, listen in and prompt and praise correct one-to-one matching and use of cues to solve new words. Prompt and praise correct page turning, and left–right direction in reading.

- Ask the children to discuss what is happening in each picture. *What is the balloon passing over? How high is it? How far might it have come? What might happen after the book finishes?*

- When the children have read the book, ask them to look at pp14–15 together. Can they recount the balloon's journey?

Returning to the book

- Encourage the children to look at the illustrations as they read. What kind are they? (Photographs). Why are photos and not drawings used for the illustrations? Use the term *illustration*.

- Read the whole book together again as a group. Model the use of correct terms like *title*, *front cover*, *illustrations*.

- Ask the children to find the words *journey*, *balloon*, *river*, *mountain*, *sea*. Point to the first letter of each word and say its sound. Ask them to suggest other words beginning with these sounds and list on a whiteboard.

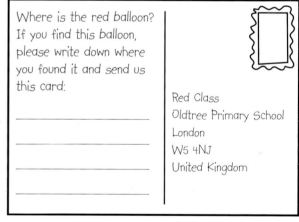

Checking and moving on

- Recap any words the children found difficult and encourage the use of initial sounds.

- Ask the children to suggest where else the balloon might have flown after the book's finish. Ask them to take it in turns to make suggestions, e.g. *The balloon goes over an island.*

- Help the children to make question-and-answer 'lift the flap', cards e.g. *What are balloons made of?*

- Send off balloons with labels to see which travels the furthest. Design school address labels to attach to a balloon.

Where is the red balloon? If you find this balloon, please write down where you found it and send us this card:

_____

_____

_____

_____

Red Class
Oldtree Primary School
London
W5 4NJ
United Kingdom

Reading more

At the Dump (Red B/Band 2B) is a non-fiction book about helping the environment.

Collins
BigCat

Red A
Band 2A

Up, Up and Away

The red balloon flies up, up and away!
Follow its journey through the sky.

ISBN 0-00-718559-6

9 780007 185597

www.collinsbigcat.com

A simple
non-fiction recount